Covenants

William Kloefkorn
and
David Lee

COVENANTS

Poems

by

William Kloefkorn and David Lee

Spoon River Poetry Press

Published by Spoon River Poetry Press, P.O. Box 6, Granite Falls, MN 56241.

Layout and cover design by Greg Boettcher
Woodcuts by Sue Cotter
Photo of William Kloefkorn by Michael Knisely
Photo of David Lee by G. Barnes

Printed by Thomson-Shore, Dexter, Michigan

ISBN: 0-944024-30-0

CONTENTS

Poems by William Kloefkorn

Poems by David Lee

COVENANTS

William Kloefkorn

–for my mother, Katie Marie,
and for my wife's mother, Gladys

COVENANT

Here is the story I might have heard,
    more likely dreamed: the woman
        after the first trimester

required by village covenant
    to compose a lullaby,
        to sing it daily then

to the gathering child, only
    from memory and in deliberate
        isolation,

the man not permitted to listen
    until the infant had been delivered
        and pronounced both whole and

welcome. And this is a ritual
    I'd go to church to live with,
        solace in the belief

that not so very far away
    always a woman sits singing her own
        creation

to that small creation breathing
    as if a delicate fish inside her,
        always not so far away

a confluence of word and of music
    flowing somehow into the ear
        of the unborn,

there to do whatever the inexplicable does
    to sustain us,
        my mother meanwhile who couldn't

3

carry a tune in a washtub
   singing as she carried the washtub
      outside to empty the rinsewater,

that same tub later
   filled with the well-wrung
      family wash, each item on the line

moving in the breeze
   like a quaint crustacean,
      each movement singing.

BUR OAK

This little nature book, Bur Oak, is yet another
I must hide from all the children.

They must not hear, not yet, such sweet seductions–
catkin, bud, pollen, stalk, acorn.

All in good time. In the fall, sap runs more slowly
through the tree. Go to sleep, my children.

Go to sleep. Meanwhile, beyond the window a squirrel
lifts in its delicate paws an acorn.

In the spring, the earth will warm again
and the tree awaken. Children,

can you hear me? I am reading you awake: A tiny root
breaks through the tip of a fallen acorn.

Can you hear it? The root burrows into the ground.
A stem appears, with bud and leaves. Children,

this baby oak will grow taller and wider every year,
given sufficient rain and sun. Once hidden, the acorn

over many moons becomes the oak you'll climb too high
in spite of all my admonitions O my children!

EARLY MORNING, LATE JANUARY

I stand on the front porch
looking to the west at a large moon
waning. Frost covers the grass, the
birch, the maple, the mountain ash.
Windless. No dog barking. I am
determined to stand here until

something more powerful than the moment
moves me. It arrives soon enough
in the form of the morning paper,
handed to me with a half-smirk
from the young girl who stammering
last week tried to tell me how much

she truly hates high school,
the paucity of her words itself
a dark-side testimony. It was her
boyfriend, she said. He dropped her
cold, and now she is inclined to detest
everything, her boyfriend at the top

of a long, long list. I inhale,
exhale. For every effect there must
surely be a cause, and so on. My
breath is a white rope soon enough
frayed to oblivion. I open the paper
to read that this time the earthquake

happened in Japan. In this best
of all possible worlds a providential
shudder has crushed too many bodies
to make a precise count possible. And
though the moon is almost full it is
not quite sufficient

for the fine print. I fold the paper
and move into the house. From the kitchen
coffee has directed its scent
heavy into the hallway. I go where rote
and comfort take me, carpet absorbing,
to a point, this congenital weight.

BACK THEN

Back then this place was a greasy spoon
    with my father's initials
        on the plate-glass

window: RK Cafe. Now, thanks to mortar
    and to time and to a long
        assortment of varying

opinions, this place is a thin cozy
    small-town library–stand
        at its center and you

can reach almost any plot or character
    you believe essential to
        your current

disposition. I settle on a collection
    of poems at about that place
        where the Bally pinball

machine entertained me after the movie
    on Saturday night. It's
        funny isn't it

how those blinking lights can't stop
    blinking, how the salt
        from that first

kiss keeps on working. Back then it was
    Edna Hatfield in the kitchen
        slapping bread dough

with the palms of her otherwise passive
    hands. At noon I hurried
        from school

to give me time for a hot-beef sandwich
and a schooner of cold
milk. Back then

the poem with its blank face rested some-
where deep in a grove
of catalpas,

waiting for something to happen so that
in turn it might likewise
happen. Now

I open the book to read that in the life
of the poet it is raining,
that he therefore

cancels the outside portion of his day,
that he adjusts readily,
finding plenty

of things to do without ever leaving the
bedroom. And because
I spent many hours

in my father's cafe I know ambiguity when
I see it, so I imagine
the poet touching

his wife awake, imagine some of the hall-
ways his touching must have
led to. My own hall-

way just now is that stretch of shelves
along the south wall
where the counter

was, its linoleum warm with porcelain cups
and the elbows of customers,
my father with a tea-

towel for an apron grinning at a story
someone who heard it
from someone else

is telling, story I can no more remember
than find in this unlikely
haven of stories.

LATE NIGHT WALK IN EARLY FEBRUARY

Through the window of an enclosed porch
I see a woman
dropping seeds fine as sawdust
into furrows made with a matchstick.

I too believe that when summer returns
I'll be there. Thus have I
covered myself with cap and coat,
gloves and my wife's dead father's scarf.

The tracks I leave in the snow are the evidence
I'll return with.

How far I walk, and to where, is anyone's guess.
But returning I notice that the porch
where the woman stood dropping seeds
stands dark.

Because my bootprints have been obscured
by the boots of others
I trust to the warm ropy tether of my breath.

Also, the sky is filled with stars,
each a sign saying This way.

I bend to gather snow to shape a snowball.
Whiteness finer than sugar
falls slowly downward,
and I stand in the cold with not even
what used to be there in my hands.

LEARNING THE DRUM

To hit something, almost anything,
   with a stick,
      to tap the stick

against the door of the granary,
   to open the door
      to enter the granary

to tap the stick against a wall
   to hear the sound
      more sharply define itself,

to inhale the yeast of the grain,
   to vary the length
      of the stick, its diameter,

to move from wood to whatever head
   reveals itself, that length
      of corrugated tin

blown last night from the roof
   of the henhouse,
      to tap the tin,

to find a companion stick,
   to try the tapping now
      with a stick in each hand,

to tap wood and tin until
   breathing itself
      becomes a cadence,

until the sticks can scarcely
   be distinguished
      from the fingers,

until the fingers become the sticks,
    fingers tapping skin,
       one's own skin

layered over bone, until this skin
    gives way to skin
       from other animals,

skin and snare beneath the drumhead
    speaking the language
       of fire, of water, of cave,

of whatever in this universe
    of flim and of flam it takes
       to keep us rolling.

SHOOTING THE SPARROWS

Just before dusk–that's the best time
   to do it, when the sparrows
     at the elevator

perch belly-heavy in the branches
   of the cottonwoods, when
     the south wind

has wilted, when the eyes of the cats
   that will carry away
     the bodies

glint as if mica among the weeds
   at the edge of the
     gravel road.

And it is not for the squeezing of the
   trigger that you
     do it, not

for the soft sudden thump as the pellet
   hits home. Nor is it
     for the blush

of bright blood on the feathers, or
   from any sense of
     necessity

to feed the cats. You are a boy
   in a little town, boy
     who woke up

this morning with another bone-on.
   When dusk moves into
     nightfall,

14

when the sparrows lose themselves in a
backdrop of darkness,
    you will go

to the drugstore for a chocolate malt.
    Sooner or later you
    will walk home,

where before going to bed to read yourself
to sleep with a copy
    of Wonder Woman

you'll shower with Lifebuoy until you are
far too aromatic to be
    resisted. Well,

what you don't know about the body's
myriad hungers
    can't hurt

you, can it? So leave it alone. You
kill the birds because
    you kill them.

GRANDDAUGHTER

How quickly she finds the ganglionic cyst
on the back of her grandmother's
hand! It is the last
plaything she'll touch
before yielding to sleep,
before the nugget that is her dream
bursts purple and golden
from the dark of its delicate skin.

I locate a copy of King James,
with spit on a Kleenex wipe the black cover
clean. It is a red-letter edition
I won for having memorized
most of Ecclesiastes. A time to rise up,
a time to lie down. I offer it
to my wife, her limpid eyes asking,
Have you lost your mind?

No. Because
it's an old cure, I tell her. You tap the cyst
gently with the Bible's spine,
and presto! at the end of three days
you can wave goodbye
to that swell pre-
cocious diversion.

Now imagine this:
You are some form of lofty deity
observing the scene–
infant asleep in her crib,
man standing before a woman
who sits with a Bible in one hand,
on the other a marble of bone. Now

imagine her tapping the tumor
gently with the holy book's
spine. And imagine her
trying to explain
to the child–awake now, her fingers
bewildered, searching–how the growth,
should it disappear,
might have gone.

WHEN THE TIME COMES

Until I was finally lifted aboard the grader
I viewed it as a toy in a Sears catalog
whose colored pages first taught me
the hierarchy of trinity: This item is good,
this one better, this one the best.

Inside the cab I blinked to see myself
as the superlative of small. Even
my father, so often lost inside his overalls,
loomed large. His size was not in fact
his size. It was instead his standing

alert behind the levers and the knobs,
the grand gargantuan wheel, his knowing
what to pull or push or turn, and when,
his grinning down at me beside him,
in our ears the husky baritone

of something distinctly more than animal.
This was my first and only venture
aboard the grader. How many times
had my father told me I could go with him
when the time comes? I had added prayer then

to my begging until at last my father's
gaunt exasperated head nodded yes.
Floating kidney and double hernia intact,
two fingers from his left hand missing,
he showed me an iron arm I might want

to cling to, he said, should the going
get rough. And the going got rough:
at a pace too slow for measurement we moved
on roads whose rocky clay the day before
had softened from a long gentle rain,

18

before and beneath us that savage yellow slug
doing its very best to shimmy us to pieces.
And we had not gone very far when suddenly
I realized that this was it--all day, forever,
I'd be standing here, gripping the iron arm,

shuddering in the heat as the grader shuddered,
my eyes at an angle watching a Kansas landscape
repeat and repeat itself, stubble into stubble,
the mongrel pup beside the silo, the white-
washed home. And I touched the nearer moment

for all its momentary worth: my father
in control, the long silver blade
turning ruts of water into a tabletop of wine
I'll drink too much of after this unending
odyssey is over, when the time comes.

SAYING IT ONCE AGAIN

Jesus is Lloyd!
    –Evan Anderson, third grade

For such a long time
Evan's contention carried a lot
of weight, made almost perfect sense.
The only Lloyd in town was Lloyd Shoemaker.
At the Champlin station I'd watch him
disappear beneath the upraised hood
of Chester Black's old Packard,
emerging finally to declare the patient
cured, better than new, restored,
fit enough to race again,
and Chester, grinning, would
cross Shoemaker's palm with a crisp new bill,
and soon enough rumor of another race
would be on almost everybody's lips,
including of course my older brother's.

So with him then I'd walk to the field
to watch the Packard run against
Delbert Garlow's high-flanked sorrel. One
hundred yards, goal-line to goal-line,
Pistol Pete Miller with his pistol
to start the race,
sidelines filled with the joyful sounds
that attend a widespread
difference of opinion.

Always the sorrel with its broad
explosive haunches
won. Always, sooner or later,
Chester returned to the Champlin station,
to Lloyd with his missing teeth and
grease for fingernails

20

to have the Packard more finely tuned. Always
Lloyd disappeared beneath the upraised hood,
and always he arose to proclaim good news.

I meanwhile sat on a green bench
with my brother, where
in tandem we folded the evening Beacon.
One by one our strongholds were falling
to the Japanese. In another month our hamlet's first fatality
would have the memory of its body
buried beside a catalpa in the cemetery.
Shortly thereafter Lloyd Shoemaker would join him.
And on consecutive Monday mornings at recess
Evan with his harelip smile, in spite
of evidence to the contrary slowly mounting,
would say it once again.

RAINFALL

*. . . mercy drops 'round us are falling,
but for the showers we plead.*
   –old hymn

When the clouds at last produce something more
than gray gloom

I follow my grandfather outside, and when he stops
between the granary and the henhouse

I stop, too, and when he reaches his speckled hand
to remove his brown felt hat

I reach for my hat, too, though I don't have one,
and gracious how cold the rain is,

how plentiful, my grandfather's face uplifted,
his old mouth in a smile

I do my best to imitate, because I believe I know
deeply what I don't,

how rainfall can relieve if not revive--not rain,
but rainfall, because

water doesn't mean shucks until it descends. So
here we stand, granary

with its coffeecan patches to our right, henhouse
with its damp and gathering congregation

to our left, beneath us dust becoming gumbo,
upon and into us

rainfall arriving at last, though arriving too late,
crops withered beyond redemption,

grandmother likewise, but even so I inhale
with my grandfather

that mix of soil and of moisture akin to something
else I'm ignorant of,

the effluvium of birth, so that for the moment
the scent is simply that

of soil and of moisture, grandmother meanwhile
lying parched on a leather duofold

beside a livingroom window, she perhaps
strong enough to see

beyond the window, perhaps alert enough
to remember the words

to the song I heard her whispering this morning
before the clouds rolled in,

mercy delinquent and insufficient, though just now
you wouldn't know it,

grandfather drenched to the bone, I drenched also
beside him,

holding in my hand the hat I never thought to bring,
neither of us dirty to start with,

both of us coming clean.

TATTOOS

–Camp Augustine, the first night

When I make a wrong turn
to find myself in the women's shower
I cannot help but notice the lovely tattoos,
how so many of them
in so many very private places
glow as if neon.

My Uncle Howard carried an American flag
on his upper left arm,
carried it with him on the second wave
at Saipan, carried it home,
carried it the rest of his life then
as he carried letters
and postcards and packages
from every corner of God's incredible earth
all over town.

When the women look up and see me
they appropriately scream. The one
with the flashiest tattoo
bites her blue towel all the way to the bone.

I blink and retreat. In the Marine Corps,
my uncle told me, retreat is a four-letter
word. Say instead retrograde movement. You
withdraw only to re-establish
a more stable line. You
understand?

He was buried in a short-sleeved shirt
with the tattoo showing.
It was showering that day, too,
gently and on all of us,
straight down.

BACK HOME, LATE MARCH

I find it impossible to be back home
    when the thunder rolls
        without thinking of God,

how thunder must be the Almighty Himself
    clearing His throat
        or cracking His knuckles,

lightning only moments before the thunder
    that sudden electric glint
        from His fire-fueled eyes.

That was the Old Testament, as all of my
    Sunday-school teachers
        taught it. Then

the New Testament in the hair and the face
    of the woman walking
        so demurely

in the rain, the rain itself a long verse
    out of Ephesians, if you'll
        forgive what the so-called

unblinded Paul said of women. I'm
    on the front porch
        swinging in a green porch swing,

hearing the thunder, watching the lightning
    and the beautiful woman
        who doesn't seem to give a damn

that the rain is making her clean. Inside,
    my wife is counting
        down the clock with her

immortal mother, both of them anxious,
    as I am, for a new ballgame
        on the old television to begin.

PINBALL

This much I know:
in the Rexall drugstore, before flippers,
Doc Bowman relied upon
touch and its second cousin,
body English.

Late into Saturday nights
I studied his liquid
movements,
in my hand a familiar issue
of Submariner, say,
some illusory text that
might yet redeem us.

Doc earned his degree in both
gin and pharmacy.
Only the sick, he said,
know the meaning of healthy.
In his spare time
he spotted nickels
with red nail polish, nickels
returned to him when the Bally man
counted the tray.

He welcomed competition, rivals
who placed their wrinkled bills
where their mouths were,
the name of the game being
Carrier, say, the lights on the ship
blinking red, white, and blue.

In a movie
whose name I can't remember
the crew of a plane
looked down upon that night's

objective, an industrial city, say,
gone suddenly theatric
with the flash and the poof
of dynamite. Thumbs up.

My town was supposed to be dry,
but Doc always managed. If
you studied him,
you could see it
behind the eyes. And it became
much worse after the machine
with the flippers arrived.
The flesh on Doc's face

wouldn't stay put,
the touch and the rhythm
diminished, neither button nor flipper
sufficient at last to save him.

I don't know what any of this,
or what anything
else, finally means. The body, body
English or otherwise, makes things
happen, or it doesn't. Lights
flash, or not, and something
poofs, or not, or pings. In the choir
sometimes the morning after
I'd move my lips silently
to Rock of Ages, say,
to hear more distinctly the
somehow sanctified sing.

APRIL

–for Alyssa

By now most of the cowlot newborn
have found and extended their legs,
by now most of the airborne critters
have changed their minds–and
by now most of the rest of us
have reached consensus:

It's about time.

I go therefore outside
for the lifting of curfews,
to hear then the sigh
and the yawn of sap
in the bur oak, the mountain ash,
the cottonwood, the linden.

It's infectious.

I go therefore inside
to attend the cradle. Wake up,
sleepyhead. We have places to go,
fat to chew, people all over the globe
to shake hands with. Wake up,
little Morpheus, little dormouse.

It's about time.

SKYLINE DRIVE NEAR CANON CITY, COLORADO

–for JLK

Not even my brother's Fleetwood bananaboat
can dispel the fear. Thus
my right hand makes the fist whose nails,
I'll discover later, will leave delicate
crimson half-moons in the plentiful meat

of my palm. My brother meanwhile
sits like a rotund rock behind the wheel,
grinning like the county's best-fed gopher.
One miscalculation and we'll go hurtling
ass over appetite into the maw

of this vast and beautiful abyss.
Funny, isn't it, how so many Christian names
sound better in Spanish. Sangre de Cristo.
Maybe, just maybe, if the fall occurs
we'll both survive it, each indentation

becoming eventually the name of a saint
on the bust of a yellowing shrine.
At the highest point we disembark
to inhale the scene. Punch-drunk,
I approach the guardrail. Because I

don't honestly know whether to relieve myself
or go blind, slowly I unclose the fist
to raise the ache of those delicate
crimson half-moons I'll discover
later into the wind.

KTSW, SUNDAY MORNING

After the Bluestem Roundup,
   after little Jimmy Dickens
      has sung the final line
         of Me and My Teddy Bear,

I insert the jack that
    connects the Catholic Church–
       and don't ask me how it
         happens,

but somewhere along the line
    I miscue the commercial,
       sending Patty-cake,
         Patty-cake, Rainbow man

deep into the heart of Father
    Lightbody's homily.
       I write an X then
         for each angry caller

until the number defies tabulation.
    Faithful listeners
       denounce me with names
         I can't find even

in the Old Testament. What can
    I say? Time and again
       I turn the other cheek,
         each time remembering

that when push comes to shove
    this earth will belong
       to the meek. But
         I quiet the multitude

only by going off-duty. Because
    it's a warm April afternoon
        I drive to the prairie
            to count all those

lovely cattle that aren't mine.
    Who was it that said
        of Kansas, love a place
            like that, and

you can be content in a garden
    of sand? I am tempted
        to pray this person
            into the lowest corner

of perdition, but this day is much
    too immaculate to be
        wasted consecrating flicker
            at the expense of flame.

I therefore park my sky-blue Chevy
    at the side of an ancient
        rock fence where
            for the longest time

I listen to the theology of space—
    where no words exist
        to nail a message to, and
            where the hem of no garment

calls (as if calling finally matters)
    to be kissed.

MEMORIAL DAY

Now the cold and persistent rain
    softens those graves
        our elders

tell us not to walk on, and
    their words because
        we hear them

as a warning heighten a day already
    high–because all
        around us

are the basement bedrooms of the
    dead, and we with our
        blossoming fists

are here to scatter posies at the
    headstones somehow
        to sweeten

them. Earlier, at the ceremony,
    a line of rifles
        sent volleys

into the darkening hearts of low-slung
    clouds. Then the rain.
        Is this what

weapons do, punch holes in those
    inverted lids
        to permit

their breathing? I have a secret.
    I loved that poor girl
        whose ailment

left her slobbering on the classroom
    floor. I give her there-
        fore all my

flowers, then wait for the others to lead
    me on. Slowly we
        serpentine

those aisles among the graves, carefully
    as if at the end it just
        might matter

we walk the line.

SATURDAY NIGHT

I walk out of Urie's barber shop
smelling like Urie's barber shop:
Sweet-Pea Talcum and Bay Rum.
I don't mention it to anyone,
but down in my heart
I know that tonight
I could have any girl in town.

Even so, I hurry home
where a garden hose hangs
from a limb on the Chinese elm.
Under a cold rope of water
I scrub until Urie's barber shop
soaks into the bunchgrass,
our only drain.

Another thirty minutes
and the orange sun will be long gone.
Windless. Now and again a leaf
the color of embarrassment
falling. Cicadas
high in a grandstand of branches
cheering me on. From
within a beehive of lather
Mind your own business! is what
I tell them.

I just want to be alone,
yet toweled and dressed
I go downtown–
to the corner booth in the drugstore,
where I sit and sit,
smelling of the powerful soap I used
to dispel the power of Urie's.
And though I don't want anything

34

of consequence to happen,
I watch the door beside
the rack of comics
closely,
waiting for it to happen.

VICTORY GARDEN, 1945

One more week, mother reminds me,
and I'll be an even dozen.

Anticipating therefore a gift
commensurate with what surely I deserve
I work most of the day at being productive,
weeding our victory garden.
It has been a small but intense commitment–
at the outset rows of beans, peas, lettuce,
radishes, onions, tomato plants, mounds
of cucumbers. Precisely how this garden
might bring victory I don't precisely
understand. But faith,
says the overweight preacher
with a wen on his forehead, can be
itself the victory.

By sundown the garden lies beautifully tended,
not so much as a single weed
among the green and ripening growth.
With water from a long blacksnake of hose
I darken the soil, I reaffirm,
I sing. Somehow

it works. The following evening
astride my bicycle, delivering the Beacon,
I announce to each subscriber that the garden
in its quaint mysterious way has yielded
imminent victory. Little Boy,
detonated at a height of 2,000 feet,
has been dropped on Hiroshima,
creating what our President calls a black rain of ruin.

I therefore harvest the onions,
tying them in bunches to hang from the roof

of the cellar. It's that musty place
I and my family retreat to
whenever the siren sounds, our faces
in a jaundice of lamplight
somehow both proud and embarrassed,
as if seeing each other again
for the very first time.

BRYCE CANYON

On our steep descent
    we stop frequently
        to exchange one form of giddiness

for another,
    until arriving finally at the base
        we stand for a long time

silent as hoodoos, hoodoos
    breathing heavily and grinning,
        hoodoos amazed not so much

at the pink impossible configurations
    as at our own brief audacity:
        we have jumped

from the body of one conclusion
    to another and have lived
        to tell it. Never mind

that the ascent lies ahead: Carpe diem
    is that darkest wine we drink
        when the skin rests

empty. Later, perusing the photographs,
    we will agree that
        chiefly through omission

does the camera lie. When I
    trip the shutter
        I exclude the ninety and

nine. So lose a sheep in this
    corkscrew universe, and
        there is not one shepherd anywhere

sufficiently divine to find it. Is
    this why, approaching
        that place at the top

where we started down, we feel
    less elected than lucky
        to be holding hands?

ON THE OREGON TRAIL
IN WESTERN NEBRASKA, 14 JULY 1993

Because the busted pod of the soapweed
smells like home
I go a final time to pillage
my grandmother's garden.

There I am, standing knee-deep
in tomatoes and onions and peavines,
there I am bending over
to disengage the shell

I'll split from stem to stern
to tongue the seeds,
to inhale the hulls of the boats
they came from, and

probably I shouldn't be doing this,
probably my grandmother both wants and needs
the fruits of her German labor, but lust,
they say, never knew guilt or conscience, so

there I am, transgressor kneeling now
in the midst of grandmother's plenty,
fists adrool with onion and pea and tomato,
and if you look closely you'll see my grandmother,

there she is, standing barefooted
on the unpainted pine of the porch,
her short thick arms as if tentacles
embracing her breasts, and though I am

much too involved to see her
I know her, know how uncommonly proud she is
of her grandson, how when she suddenly shouts
she'll be calling no more to him than

to all those others from the old countries,
brothers and uncles, fathers and mothers and aunts,
and if you look again closely you'll see
both him and his grandmother,

there they are, the thief
and the prodigal, both grinning,
a crack through the center of the sepia snapshot
unable to disjoin the blood in their mutual hands.

EATING THE APPLE

With an old Uncle Henry in one hand
and a day-old jonathan in the other
I go outside to the south porch
for Sunday school.

Autumn with its descending leaves
rises taller and leaner than ever.
With the longer blade
I quarter the apple, with the same blade
deliver the tart fruit slice by slice,
and slowly, onto a receptive tongue.

Deuteronomy returns to tell me that
after I have besieged the city
and have taken it,
I must cut down
only those trees not bearing fruit.

A jay with something other than
music on its mind
trembles a high limb on the mountain
ash. With wood from the non-bearing trees
I am to build bulwarks
to defend my city against others
who most surely shall fashion wooden
ramrods to besiege it.

A sudden brisk breeze
unswaddles the black walnut.
I finish the apple, click home the knife-
blade. Yesterday, in the sweet heavy heft
of Swanson's orchard, my granddaughter
chose and picked an apple
pretty much the color of her
wind-chilled face. With my Uncle Henry

I peeled it, with a silver blade
sliced and delivered it piece by piece,
and slowly, into the palm of her out-
stretched hand.

From each of the four great directions
I can hear the tolling of bells,
and I remember how the fruits in Leviticus
are not to be eaten for three full years,
how during that time the fruits
are to be considered
uncircumcised.

From the porch then
I kick a path into the center
of the newly-fallen leaves. I inhale
deeply. The bells fade
into palpable silence. Because
there is no wall between us
I can see my neighbor
indulging a toddy, and suddenly
I do not hate anyone in particular.

MOTHER, POLISHING MY SHOES

How can I ever have what enormous cheek it must take
to tell her not to do it, to put my bare foot down,
to say that I am much too old and thus too wise

to be lying here on the couch while my mother,
polishing my shoes, rattles on and on
about the non-adventures of another day? Truth is,

she is never more beautiful than just now, and
always (I'm going to say it) she is beautiful. With
two fingers she applies the polish, brown as

buckeyes, rubs it in, rubs slowly in circles slowly,
her eyes above the shoes impossible for my own eyes,
no more indolent than prodigal, not to meet. She has

covered her lap with an old blue cotton towel, the one
that for much of my life I dried myself on, and
what she is saying is somehow cotton, too, her left hand

meanwhile swallowed by the shoe, two fingers on her red
rough other hand moving slowly in circles slowly,
preparing the shoes for the shine that I know already

will restore them. In another life I went with Grand-
mother to a tent revival. Ropes tight almost
as catgut on a fiddle to steady the tentpoles. Saw-

dust. A woman wide as all creation at the piano. The
corpulent preacher's eyes popped very nearly out
as flailing a huge black dog-eared Bible he spoke

of the imminence of Armageddon. Next month, perhaps.
Next week. Tomorrow. Tonight, as we lie sleeping!
How the aisles filled then with those not decisive enough

earlier to have earned a space to kneel on at the altar.
In the morning before I put them on I'll lift the new-
shined shoes to smell them, polish

joined to leather joined to the scent of my mother's
effort, her words without saying it saying it: O
give me the grace to live long enough to touch again

that other part of living!–two fingers rubbing slowly
in circles slowly, everything pointing brightly
as that first star points to another day.

AFTER THE DIVORCE

Playing tackle football
on buffalo grass beside the Baptist church
I lose my Tom Mix Secret Decoder Ring.

Don't worry, I tell my buddies, the ring
glows in the dark. I'll find it
when the sun goes down.

Only Galen the quarterback
will go with me. In the swelter
of a mid-August night

we do not find the ring–nothing brighter
than an occasional lightning bug
sluggish above the gridiron.

Later, in the Rexall drugstore,
I treat Galen to a chocolate malt. We stand
flanking the pinball machine,

watching the lights on the Bally
blink and ping,
admiring the smooth gyrations put forth

by the hips of the local aficionado,
Fuzzy Bateman. Around midnight
we start home.

In the darkness, ring or no ring,
you sometimes discover who your true
friends are. Tonight they are Galen,

who walks me to the back porch,
who sits with me most of the rest
of the night, both of us speaking of loss

and of gain and of football,
above us the glow of bodies neither
one can name.

46

BY LAMPLIGHT

In darkness, by touch and by taste,
her breasts are identical twins.
What might they be by lamplight?

I imagine Grandfather
having trimmed the lampwick
touching Grandmother, she having
turned back bedsheets yet
stiff with starch. I imagine
Grandmother's long grey hair immeasurably
wild against a feathered pillow. Yes,
they are no longer young. I imagine
how a butterfly quilt secures their ankles,
how by lamplight their bodies must have
flickered and gleamed,
how her breasts must have heaved
mysteriously in light and in shadow,
Grandfather's hands, his lips,
delicate in their delicate measurements.

This is what I want to say:
I am yet my grandparents'
grandson. In fantasy then
I fill the lamp with oil, I trim the wick,
strike the match, replace the globe,
adjust the flame. In halflight
the yellowed bedroom wavers. Lying
on her back on a flowered sheet
she covers her breasts with mature
and adequate hands. Yes,
I am no longer young. Yet beside her
I am the infant that in its moments
of sweetmilk and of tongue thank God
I have always been.

47

THE GREAT DEPRESSION

In the treehouse at dusk
I finger the old Barlow that
earlier in the day
I swapped with my buddy Carlos
sight-unseen for.

The blade is dull,
but you can bet not half as dull
as the blade on the old Barlow that
my buddy Carlos
earlier in the day received
sight-unseen from me.

When before long total darkness
settles among the branches
I'll trade even-up with God:
my belief in Him
for grit enough
to outlast indeterminate sorrow.

Now here's another unlikely deal,
thanks to this Great Depression:
my sister sent away to Timbuktu
to live with Grandma.

Tonight the moon will be a perfect
half. I know this because
last night it so nearly was.
I watched it climb on wavering rungs
until my neck no less
than the lower half of me
could not stop aching.

Eventually a cloud will obscure the moon,
eventually a west wind (guttural

against invisible leaves, my suddenly
lonely mother's lonely voice) will
insist: One day
you'll look back at this and wonder
why in the world you ever created
such a terrible fuss.

A west wind rises.
I count by ones
until all of the numbers are gone,
then I count again.

BATHING IN THE LOUP

Bare-assed and vulnerable,
green jon-boat
tethered to a cottonwood
thus far not molested
by beaver,
I bathe myself
until the fresh bar of Ivory

loses the letters of its identity.
If a goddess should happen along,
if I should look up
to see her watching me,
would I be within my mortal rights
to strike her forever blind?

Sand fine almost as sugar
gives way beneath my feet.
Sac and horn float on the water
as if bobber and bait.
I extend the lathering
to include the face, the hair.
Eyes closed,

I give myself over to movement,
this body as if the unwieldy log
that because its resistance is low
sooner or later will get there.
When eventually I rise,
when eventually my legs are steadied
against the current,

I will shake the river from my hair
to see already a half moon
skirting the clouds,
and trusting its light

I'll return to the boat
and the cottonwood, to the spot
where the goddess might have stood,

where I will build the fire.

BACK HOME, LATE AUGUST

A crooked line of catalpas
forms the north boundary
of the cemetery,
their beans in a slant
of three-quarter moon
hanging long and skinny and green.
Anybody here named Legion?
Anybody here want to sell a Studebaker?

At the ball park the Bulldogs
have rolled over and played dead,
defeat like the finger of silence
on the lips of a host of cicadas.

In a window at the Rexall drug
a clock with a full well-lighted face
yawns like a child in church. No,
its hands don't appear to give a damn
what time it is.

Parked in a Chevrolet
at the center of a shelterbelt
the young woman shares with the young man
her last stick of Black Jack gum.
Music on the Philco
tells them how easy it is
to love each other forever.

Tomorrow morning the weekly reading
will derive from Ephesians:
For by grace are ye saved through faith;
and that not of yourselves.

When the young man rolls down his window,
the shelter releases itself

thickly aromatic into the delicate confines
of the front seat.
For the longest time the couple will sit
together without touching, breathing
in and breathing out.
Breathing in.

LAST VISIT

This nursing home stinks. Chicken
feathers. *Wet* chicken feathers.
My grandfather in blue overalls
sitting on the edge of an
unmade bed. My grandfather

looking up from the floor to see me
standing in front of him,
his mouth calling me by my brother's
name. John. My brother. Who
cut an artery many years ago

while swimming in a sandpit two miles
east of town. Red. O
red is the color of my brother's
blood. And spurt. Spurt
is what the blood does as it

leaves the artery. Behind his eyes
my grandfather seems to be thinking.
Spurt. I found the relevant
pressure point and applied
pressure. The spurt became a trickle,

a red thread down the fishbelly white
of my brother's arm. My grandfather
smiles. This nursing home stinks.
This southcentral Kansas nursing home
smells like feathers. Chicken

feathers. *Wet* chicken feathers. Chicken
hanging upside-down on the clothes-
line, chicken decapitated, chicken
soon to be scalded and plucked clean
and disemboweled and dismembered,

each member coated thickly with flour,
then skillet-fried and served
to a family too graciously alive
ever to be otherwise. My brother
white as flour from the loss of

blood. Red. O red is the color. And
my grandfather sitting in blue overalls
on the edge of an unmade bed
in this southcentral Kansas nursing home
that smells like wet feathers, that

stinks. John, he says, Johnny. Is that you?

ROLLING OUR OWN

–for Jack Ernst

Adrift on a backyard of late-spring bunchgrass
  my neighbor stands rolling a cigarette,
    his body down almost to the bone

leaning slightly into a soft mid-morning
  wind. Because I don't ask
    he tells me: he has always considered

the shaping of one's own smoke to be
  an art form, has always dreamed
    of mastering the form. Funny, isn't it,

he says, how the mind works? At such an hour
  shouldn't it be contemplating
    something more eternal than tobacco

from a sack of Bull Durham rolled perfectly
  as a brand new length of chalk?
    Because I don't respond

he does: No–at such a time
  the mind goes its own cockeyed and thus
    most human way. So I join him, I who

don't smoke, either, I who until just recently
  believed that melanoma was a song, a melody,
    until my neighbor's body sang the song,

song of the melanoma, until the song
  took his flesh down almost to the bone,
    at which moment I do my level best to join him,

fingers fumbling to contain tobacco
  inside a tube of tissue,
  until my neighbor grinning brings forth

two cold and beautiful beers,
  whereupon we retire to the porch to dismiss
  all thoughts of black pigmented tumors–instead,

to cough outrageously in unison, to bask becalmed
  in the perfect because perfectly artless rays
  of the rising sun.

GUTS

No guts, no sausage.
       –Socrates

It's what my father says
    I didn't have enough of
        when Junior Ballard came hurtling

hellbent at me on the playground.
    How can I explain that sometimes
        not even guts can counter-

balance blind misfortune? Junior
    caught me off-guard
        with a wild right cross, that's

all, but father only shakes and
    shakes his head. I
        had used my hands

as a bowl until it overflowed, then
    remembered to pinch the nostrils.
        Jesus, this is the first time

I have seen my own red blood in such
    abundance. Will mother ever
        be able to take it

from this shirt? In almost fifty years
    my father will be laid open
        by a drunk too ephemeral

to distinguish green from red. Blood
    stringy almost as sinew is what
        my brother and I will wring

58

from the dark dark cotton of his personal
belongings. Until then I
        entertain a myriad of doubts:

Was it lack of guts that prevented me
        from ignoring the blood to launch
        a counter-offensive? Is the

untapped nose, no less
        than the untapped life, worth
        having? My father will be driving

with his girlfriend on a warm
        and lazy Sunday afternoon. He
        will be eighty-two. He will

wait for the light to change. He will
        never see to know what it is
        that hits him.

GEESE

I hear them honking
   before I see them,
      a low-flying V

going wherever V's go
   when the sap in the ash
      gives way to gravity.

And I am tempted to draw
   some natural-world
      conclusion,

to say that the birds
   know something the rest
      of us don't, and maybe

they do, though my mother
   at eighty-three
      takes her cue each year

from the first frost, she
   and her boyfriend then
      as if a skein of two

on the wing for Texas. So
   it seems to me that
      the natural world

and the other one
   considerably overlap.
      I hear them honking

before I see them, my mother
   and her boyfriend
      in a blue pickup

lifting off, the motion
of my mother's out-
stretched arm

as natural as any natural
world can be
in its act of going.

AFTERNOON IN OCTOBER

About the only thing
    that interests me now,
        my father said then,

is the weather. The
    previous year he had
        given up on Scotch,

his nightly shot
    no longer helping him
        into sleep.

Shortly thereafter he took
    an additional pledge:
        no more left

turns. Ironic, isn't it,
    that the driver who
        killed him

was so supremely drunk
    it never occurred to him
        to brake left,

it never having earlier
    occurred to him
        to acknowledge the color

red. On a clear bright
    windless afternoon
        in late October

I sit alone on a pine-slatted
    bench, thinking about
        my father,

about what finally came
to interest him,
about those vows

he gave himself so briefly
before that moment
of prodigal

impact. And about time, how
it means everything and
nothing. At my right

a bur oak cannot contain its
secret: it wants
to be climbed into,

it wants me to detach myself
to do the climbing,
it wants to hold me

as if the son that somehow
slipped away
in the arms of its

dark and haunted branches.

MAGGIE'S POND, LATE AUTUMN

Why is the duck unable
to lift itself from the water?
Its wings appear adequate,
yet their threshing, however
violent, cannot lift its body
from the surface
of the spring-fed pond.

I move to watch it
from a closer and higher angle,
wings of the duck meanwhile
slapping the water
with a spastic cadence
only the truly mad might dance to.

When the cadence slows,
and the wings reflect what can
only be inferred as a dense fatigue,
I see the turtle, its mouth a vise
on the duck's defenseless leg,
its dark enormous body
moving in a slow steady motion
downward.

Until the duck, absolutely spent,
its flat wings on the water its
last resistance,
sinks feather to feather, the eyes
in the head at the end
of the not quite interminable neck
more open than open,
more incredulous, it seems,
than afraid.

I stand watching the ravaged water
heal itself, cool spring water
no less inviting than apparently
undisturbed. Changing then
from bloodbait to a lure
I cast the jitterbug
precisely where I intend–under
an overhang of willow,
the little splash of the lure
spooking a bird with lovely dollops
of flame into orange on its
suddenly adequate wings.

COUNTING THE COWS

Because earlier in the day I walked the fencelines
I know that none has escaped or wandered off,
and though I realize that should the count fall short

I'd have two options, count again or shrug my shoulders,
I go to the field to count them, anyway, knowing as I do
that counting is itself sufficient cause for counting,

something sweet in the accumulation, you understand,
and if the count should complement the ledger
how much sweeter then the effort. And if the count

falls short, as occasionally it does? Always I choose
to shrug the shoulders, my consolation more than equal
to potential loss, the credit being this: that I have

seen and have inhaled, at dusk, the lovely bulk of cow,
that its path returns no less than takes me away from
home. All of this is what my grandfather in the course

of an autumn morning more or less informs me. We are
in that room where Grandmother died, her body at last
a fencepost under a hand-tied quilt. And before the sun

quite drops behind its hill I'll be moving in my father's
familiar Chevrolet, gravel pelting its underside
like the rain that so far not even prayer has been able

to induce. Dusk. At my left I see the darkening silhouettes
of grandfather's cows, their heads lowered as if ritual
into the occasional nourishment

of bunchgrass. One. Two. Three. All there, each cud
in a land of milk and of honey, you understand,
and accounted for.

LUNAR ECLIPSE

Though I was here
somewhere in the universe
I missed it, I managed somehow
to overlook it, probably because
I had better things to do,

though just now
I can't remember what they were,
important as surely they must have been,
our Christmas tree, for example,
appearing suddenly inside the old garage
because this year I ordered one over the phone,
ordered it from an organization that,
though Christian,
promised to deliver,

so inside the old garage,
looking for something else,
I stumble across the tree, five feet
of soft pine needles, and quickly I forget
what I was looking for, I grab a handsaw
and prepare the tree for its metal stand,
which I go to the basement to search for,
which I return to the old garage to find,
until the tree rises from the stand
substantial as if it grew there,

or more likely I missed it
because that part of me symbiotic
wants to hear of it from someone else,
someone with big eyes who adores looking up,
someone who knows how to fashion importance,
how to hold something cosmic
in the palm of the hand,
how to deliver it then, as if something
that matters between us, into mine.

READING THE COFFEE GROUNDS

Reading the coffee grounds
she tells me what not even my list
of unlikely predictions holds: After
his death by impact
your father will return
to guide you through.

Of course I don't believe her.
She is no more authentic than was the phrenologist in Tijuana
who called the sudden rise on my head
the bump of reverence. Sweet Jesus!
Can you imagine? The simple
truth is this: Less than one hour
earlier I had tripped over my own
wayward feet in the barroom bathroom,
my skull a ramrod
against the thick wooden door.

Yet tonight my father
turns right at the first stop-sign
north of the Baptist church
and drives himself in his yellow Fairlane
smack into the bedroom
where I lie rigid as a fencepost,
every ounce of my waning body
resisting sleep. Tuned her myself,
he says, the Fairlane at idle
humming Rock of Ages. Nothing
I might say will ever convince him
of the truth: That he never once
tuned an automobile without
further untuning it. So
I remain silent, though I notice
that the car's interior has been
refurbished, not so much as a single

blooddrop on the dash, the steering
wheel, the upholstery.

How did you do it? I ask, meaning
how did you manage so thoroughly
to eliminate the blood.
But he doesn't understand. He speaks instead
of plugs and of coils and of wires,
talks until I become almost convinced
that in death he knows something
he never knew in life. That's
how I did it, he concludes, and grinning
he revs the motor and is gone.

Late into the night
I listen to the melodies of night—
cidada and the nearby neighbors
with little of contention
in their throats,
and the cough and the hum
of many motors, each with someone
going somewhere, each
with the delicate resonance
of my father's name.

CHURCH

My girlfriend scolds me
　　because I lifted an offering plate
　　　　from the Baptist church.

Tonight, the plate overflowing
　　with fresh-buttered popcorn,
　　　　we sit listening to the radio,

waiting for Joe Louis to say something
　　before he climbs into the ring
　　　　to throttle Tami Mauriello.

She asks, Why did you? She says,
　　I don't want to have children
　　　　with a common thief. How

can I explain to her my affinity
　　for such well-turned mahogany?
　　　　Not to mention

the sense of balance derived from
　　taking out instead of
　　　　putting in. When the popcorn

is almost gone I can see what I knew
　　already, that the bottom
　　　　of the plate is lined

with magenta felt. Two-thirds
　　into the opening round
　　　　Louis leaves Mauriello

senseless against the ropes. My girl
　　sits straight-backed
　　　　on the sofa, licking butter

70

from her salty lips. I pull a crumpled
one-dollar bill from my pocket,
        drop it softly

into the plate. Eldonna, whose breasts
are identical twins, shakes
    her head: she shall

not be purchased at any price. What
I want to whisper into her
    delicate ear is what

I cannot muster the courage to whisper:
Because I do not deserve to be
    forgiven, I ask only this:

forgiveness.

SUSTAINING THE CURSE

Rona, a woman who may have lived on the shore of the Kaipara Harbor, went to get water because her children were crying at night. The moon disappeared behind a cloud and Rona cursed it because she stumbled in the darkness--so the moon came down and took her up into the sky, where she is still to be seen on its face.
–Maori legend

And still to be heard are those cries
from so many bewildered children,

many of them nonetheless destined to
survive. Rona, you were right to have cursed

but wrong to have cursed the moon.
Did the moon obscure itself? No,

it was the cloud that provided the
obfuscation–or, if not the cloud,

the breeze from the west that
moved the cloud, or the low-pressure

belt just off the shoreline that
shaped the breeze that blew the cloud

that obscured the moon. Even so, moon
in its loftiness should have seen

what you were about, what you intended,
in turn should have done whatever

moon might do to enlighten. But no,
moon takes you instead to its face,

giving you life everlasting while
so many bewildered children lie

crying for water. Well, let them
cry. Let many of them survive. And let

some of these in their own eventual
darknesses sustain the curse.

COVENANTS

David Lee

for Jim Brummels
for Ken Brewer
for Katharine Coles
for Russell Martin
for David Clewell
for Bill Holm
for Richard Shelton,
with considerable affection
and enthusiasm

LABOR

Nehemiah 6:3
Ecclesiastes 9:10

Harold Rushing died
so we had to change the way
we talked about him

they taken and given the sorriest funeral
I ever saw for his wife Suetta to listen to
him looking terrible in his box on a Thursday
the sun shining outside while that preacher
went on about the glories of the churchhouse
and the love of the lard for the collection plate
never sed nothing about
how that man would rather farm than eat
the week's work he'd try to get done
in a day when he didn't have to be embarrassed
in there laying down
in front of people
with a dam necktie on

I seen him of a summer
on a tractor holding his dinner
in a bucket and a waterjug in a tow sack
hanging on the fender in his other hand
7 butterfingers in his shirt pocket
36 hours without no sleep
six and 1/2 days on a week
till he had to drive up to town
to be a Campbellite elder on Sundays
where he could get some rest
if they didn't ask him to offer prayer

he broken his arm on a power takeoff
this hired hand had to get his wife

to call Doc Kitchens to come out to the north field
to set that bone
he sed he didn't have no time to wait
kept on working with his hand
flopping like a blue flag on his wrist
with his handkerchief wrapped around
so he wouldn't have to look at it
Doc Kitchens had to go out there
and he had a horrible time catching him
on his tractor because he'd been drinking whiskey
it was a Saturday
and he didn't have no appointments
for breaking bones that day
Harold Rushing stopped working long enough
so he could tie it in a splint with doctor tape
Doc Kitchens sed let's go to town
put that all in a cast with the Xray
he sed not today I have work to do
I'll bring it in right before churchtime tomorrow
Doc Kitchens sed only if you come to the office
I aint putting it on
in the churchhouse parking lot

wasn't a week later changing
sucker rod on that windmill
out to the east gate by the pasture
with the cast on when the wind come up alone
thrown him off on the othern
where the bone stuck through
both arms ruint then
back on that tractor next morning
sed Suetta and the hired hands would have to:
carry buckets
shovel
hammer nails

78

pick up eggs
and milk cows
but he could do the rest
they'd have to get by with the inconvenience

had his 1st heart attack
when he's about 56 years old more or less
Doc Kitchens sed Harold Rushing
you got to slow down
let them hired hands do more of that heavy work
you're posta be paying them to do
or that heart's gone give it up on you
you got to start treating things better
Harold Rushing sed it lives with me
it'll have to keep up best it can
Doc Kitchens sed you haven't learned
one thing for being alive have you?
he sed yessir Doc Kitchens I have
I learnt if I walk slow through that door
on the way out of here and it's swinging
it'll bump me on the butt
and that aint gone happen today
I'll see you after the sermon on a Sunday
so you can get your sins and equity paid up
brang me the bill and I'll pay it then
if I don't have to listen to no more today

he died when he's 62
in his field bucking bales with a 18 year old
hired hand driving truck for wages
of a heart attack that Doc Kitchens
sed was such a stroke it could of busted in 2
he torn the front of his shirt off
beat bruises and knuckle spots
all on his chest where he tried to get to it

they sed he'd of strangled that heart to death
if he could of got his hands on it
but it wasn't enough time left to break through
Harold Rushing didn't have no use for nothing
that tried to quit before the work got done
on a day when the Lord's sun was shining

PSALM WRITTEN AFTER READING CORMAC McCARTHY AND TAKING A THREE HOUR CLIMB TO THE TOP OF PINE VALLEY MOUNTAIN

Laughter is also a form of prayer
–Kierkegaard

Right here, Lord,
tether me to my shadow
like a fat spavined mule
stuck sideways in tankmud
bawling for eternity

At midnight
when the stars slip their traces
and race the moon like wild horses
to their death in the darkness
let my hoarse song twine with the nightwind

May the bray
of today's laughter fall
like a pitchey topbranch from a tall yellow pine
straight down like winter sleet
to the mountain's bent and trembling knees

HOUSEDOGS

Not louder shrieks to pitying heaven are cast
When husbands, or when lapdogs breathe their last
—Pope, The Rape of the Lock

Ollie McDougald when I set down
at the counter to have coffee sed
he didn't want to talk about it
I seen he's down in the mouth sez whar?
he sed it aint nothing to speak of
I let it go and watched
while he stirred his coffee without no sugar
or milk in it with his spoon studying
sed finally if it's any of your business
it's that goddam fycet
my brother-in-law by marriage taken
and given to my wife she name Sweetie
now that sonofabitch lives in the house
all day and at night in our bed
it's about ruirnt my whole life
marriage done shot to hell
and dogshit all over the yard
what am I posta do?
B. L. Wayburn running coffee and cash register
listening in sez it aint nothing
about all this I don't know
so you curious you just axe me

I been married 3 times had 9 dogs
2 of them in the house by 2 wormern
I'll tell you now free of charge
2 things you can set your watch to
and live a life by if you want
1st is a married wormern can only love a thing
if she can pity it and run over it
which is why they let them things

82

set in their laps smelling them
watching T V in the house
whenever they scratch on the door to get in
and the 2nd is what your daddy
should of told you in high school that
a wormern's love is like morningdew
sparkles like a diamond in a goat's ast
it might land on a red garden rose or a turd
it won't known the difference
you better make yourself accustom
she ever has to choose between you
and that shiteater you just as well
get on down the gravelway kicking roadapples
one of them might be dew wet
remember it caint necessarily help it
her and it just likes the shine
so all you can do is scrape off your shoes
come on in and set down
try to outlive it and not get anothern
that dog's as permanent and official
as Judge Parker in his courthouse
you want to stay married
make you a compromise and do it her way
that's all there is to it

PREACHER

In 1956 Baptists got a new preacher
Reverend Pastor Brother Strayhan
from the Southern Tennessee preacher school seminary
he had a Bible they give him
for graduating had about 40 ribbons
marking his page number
hanging out the back
ever color you could imagine
after he'd been there about a year
still tell them about how
they didn't appreciate him enough
because he was awarded them ribbons
for being outstanding in his field
one day Mizrez Bouchier
who was old enough to not care no more
sed after church she wished
he'd go back and stand
out in his field some more
she had enuf of him arredy

he'd preach swinging that thing
round like a Chinaman's kite
by the end the sermon
he'd took out the ribbons marking spots
all worked up to give the invitation
swung it so hard oncet
them ribbons chopped the top
off a incarnation in the pulpit flowerpot

he loved to preach on how
he got calt by the Lard to be his servant
when he's only 16 years old
met his lovely wife that same summer
my mama sez she figgered he's right
all boys that age get calt

84

some of them even on the telephone
but she thought the Lord
got a wrong number that time
we all scrut up now and then

he had about 9 kids
sed it was the Lard's will
oldest one not even 12
his wife looked like a inner tube
without about 1/2 its air
you'd hear her in the grocery store
2 aisles over
her feet drug so
she's wore out not even 30
and known it was her
before you saw her
by the sound

even if he got his preacher pay
and a house and a car
and his electric and water
with all them kids he thought
it wasn't enough to get by on
ever 3d Sunday the sermon
was on the collection plate
and the bread on the water
he'd go round town
asking all the business for a preacher discount
wouldn't buy nothing in a store
if they didn't mark it down for him
when they didn't
he could make them sorry for it
he'd find some way to get it
into 1 of his sermons
whole churchhouse would go

somewhere's else after that
whether they believed it or not
his kids got in the pitchershow
1/2 price and free meals
at the school lunchroom
and the ball games without paying
because it was the Lard's will

so oncet he went to Lela's cafe
for supper with his whole family
stood there at the counter
before he'd set down
sed how much is your menstral discount
to eat there
customers listening 2 waiting to pay
sez I need at least 20 percent?
Lela sed whar? she wasn't even
a Baptist but a Presbyter
sez my family and I get discounts
because of I'm the Baptist Reverent
of up to 1/2 at most places
one of the people eating there
Clovis Robinson I think
sed yesmaam that's a fact
he's a Baptist deacon
had to back him up without no choice
wasn't nothing she could do
everbody watching to see
if they'd all walk out
Lela sed set down
I'll do my 20 percent 1 time
all them kids standing there
with their mouths hanging open
3 of them didn't even
have their britches zipped up

he order tunafish sandwiches
and a glass of water
for all them kids because it was cheapest
fried chicken for his wife
because that was most for the money
and told this waitress
to bring him a steak to eat
how do you want that cooked? she sed
Scriptural he sed
she sed what?
he sez well done
my good and faithful servant
leant back and grint
proud of hisself like he thought
she ought to brang him a dish of icecream
for free for thinking up that

Lela heard it
hollered through the winder
from the cash register to the cook
whole cafe listening
fix that preacher's kids hamburgers
and french fries
make his wife shrimps and whitefish
put him a steak on
from off the bottom of the pile
I'll pay the different
cook sez how he want that steak?
she yelled scriptural
burn that sonofabitch to hell
he never did come back there
to eat again after that
and it never hurt Lela's business
not even 1 bit

CIGARETTES

Now Roy Bob Jamerson
had a heart attackt about 6 months
before he died or seven
Doctor told him he had to give it up
the smoking or he'd have anothern
he sed how much good will it do?
Doctor sez it'll add days or weeks
mebbe months tacked on the end
like fourth of July cotton mill bonus

Roy Bob Jamerson sed bullshit
it aint worth it
that wasn't enough to buy
two bottles of cheap whiskey
he had this in law
by marriage been quitting smoking
for moren 5 years and he's a dam mess
with his whole life because of it
goes out to drink a drink
he'll have to have a smoke or 2
when he gets home his wife
which is my wife's cousin
rattles like a chainsaw
when she smells it on him
they'll holler till he's had enough
slams the screendoor
goes to get drunk and smoke, all her fault
he'll take up with some womern
spend the whole night out
testing the back springs in his car
next day use up all his time
thinking a excuse to his wife
he'll go have a drink to help
there he goes again needing a smoke
sed it was one time
he didn't get hardly no sleep

for a month trying to quit smoking
and it was a terrible experience

I haven't got no time
to lose sleep he sed and I'm too old
to get drunk and chase wormen all night
so he told his daughter right then to go
buy him some Chesterfields or Pell Mells
make sure they given her
some matches to light them with

he smoked 2 or 3 packs of cigarettes
for the rest of his life
every day before he died
and then it wasn't a heart attackt
but the emphysema
he sed it was because
when he was a boy
he had to clean out the chicken house
by hisself all them years
without no help
all that new ammonia in the air
ate up the inside his lungs
ruint him
he wasn't never the same
smoking didn't have nothing to do with it

his brother sed that was a fact
but it wasn't their fault
he was the oldest
got started by hisself from their daddy
he had his own way to do it all
oncet he had his mind set on a thing
whether it was chicken shit or smoking cigarettes
he'd stay with it till he finished
Roy Bob had some principles to live his life by.

WHISKEY

Leonard Askins was a bad one
to drink even before he went deaf
he'd work the afternoon shift
for one place and the next
then go get drunk most of the night
sed it was the only way
he could stand to put up
with working that hard all day
until he lost his hearing
he must of figured if he couldn't hear
nobody else could either
he went on social security
so he could be drinking full time

way back before that
he took the pledge oncet for good
had this boy in the third grade
that had a class party
for animals name Albert Askins
but he didn't have no pet to bring
they's in between dogs
cat run off or got run over
that afternoon his mama got tored
of saying no and hearing about it
some more so she finally took him
up to Wackers dime store
bought him a turtle with a black shell
out of the fish tank for 50 cents
sed now you don't talk about it again
took it home and he sed he was satisfied
made a turtle pen with a baking dish
soaked some water in it
on the kitchen table
left it there when he went to bed

next morning there was a bellering
like a hurricane bit off his ear
woke Leonard Askins up
he hadn't come in till real late drunk
and he'd told them kids
it wouldn't be no hollering in the house
on mornings when he'd been up
working hard all night
they had to let him sleep
he didn't tell them he was drunk
but they could smell the whiskey
he come out to the kitchen
sez what in the hell is going on?
I'm about to loose my patience
boy sez somebody done stoled my turtle
daddy I name Freddy for the animal party
his mama sed it was on the table
we put it right there last night
boy sez it was on the table
somebody done stoled it
now I caint go to the party

Leonard Askins sed I don't care
about no goddam turtle
I told you not to yell in this house
when it's real people sleeping
ever one of you get out of this house right now
find you something on the way
a snake or a frog or there's dogs everwhere
you can catch you one for the day
get out of this kitchen
or I'll whup your butt till your nose bleeds
started to take his belt off
all them kids hit that door
gone without no breakfast

hollering like roosters
Leonard he could be mean
some of them didn't even have
their shoes put on
it wasn't worth the chance

he sed to his wife only thing
on that table last night
was a cold biscuit in a pie plate
with some tuna fish sandwich in it
that I ate for supper
when I got home
it wasn't nothing else there
she hung her mouth open
turnt and looked out the window
never did say no more about it

3 days later he was sitting
on the furniture drinking a coldbeer
when he set straight up
hollered oh my lardgod all mighty
sed you could of hammered hub caps
on his eyes
he taken and thrown that coldbeer
right against the wall
run in to the kitchen sed
you tell them kids of yours
first one ever finds something alive
tries to bring it here again
he'll have to have another place to be
if he's not dead by then when I'm through
it won't be no more animals of no kind
here never again inside this house
took all the beer out of the frigerator
pourn it down the sink

had a bottle of 4 Roses hid
that he shot with a pistol
sed he wouldn't never drink
another drop of whiskey
as long as he lived
and he meant it by god
never took a taste of it
for over two weeks

rest of his life you could almost tell
when he thought of tunafish
he wouldn't have a can of it
in his house for no reason
if he ever seen or worst smelt it
he'd retch and gag
like a dry hand pump
it was a lesson to be learnt
that boy Albert never drank whiskey once
turnt out to be a deacon
for the churchhouse
married a fat womern that taught Sundayschool
sed her favorite lesson
was Jesust miracles
but not the one about the water and wine
she didn't believe in that one
she loved to tell them kids
how he fed all them multitudes
made sandwiches for them
out of 5 little loaves of bread
and them 3 tunafishes.

NEIGHBORS

Bullards and the Bloodworths lived
down the street from each other both ways
had about 9 kids more or less
nobody ever got a good count
on them Bloodworths so it could of been more
like a whole backyard full of hens
and ducks chasing grasshoppers
it was always bloody nose, skinned knee
I'm gone tell my mama she'll whup your ast
even after the sun went down
you could hear Fibber McGee 4 blocks away
everybody had it cranked up so loud
to drown them out in the whole neighborhood
especially when they ever got on the churchhouse

they'd line up acrost the street from each other
take turns hollering
        my mama sed yall aint going to heaven
when you died
        well my mama sez onliest ones there
are the Baptists
        my mama sed Jesustchrist he never
heard of no Baptistchurch
        well he goddam never went to no
Penneycosted
                not one without no flags especially
        my mama sed them is idolarties and you're
a sonofabitch
        my mama sez your mama is full of shit

then they'd thrown rocks
until one or anothern would call them
in for suppertime

one July when it was hot
Billy Joe Bullard run home
told his mama Rosemary Bloodworth
sed her mama told her
he couldn't never be no sunbeam for Jesust
Mizrez Bullard she had it
taken off her aporn
thrown it on the floor
slammed the screendoor when she left
went down the street
she's so mad you could hear
her feet in the gravels
hollered Lucille Bloodworth
out of her house
sed what did you say to that one girl
about my Billy Joe?
it was just as hot
in Lucille Bloodworth's house that day
she sed I never sed one thing
about that boy of yourn
you keep him at home
if you don't want him in my yard
is he the one has dogshit on his shoes?
Mizrez Bullard sed did you say
Christjesust never wanted my boy?
we don't have no dog
othern sez that boy never been truly warshed
in the blood of the lamb

that done it
Mizrez Bullard swung on her
like a cement mixer
next thing they both spitting
slapping and clawing
then they grabbed hair

95

street looked like 4 of Bus Pennel's hounds
slunk down it looking for a place
to lay down and die of mange in the crawl space
under somebody's back porch
hair and blood and snot all over
both of them screaming like a razorblade
just like 2 hogs fighting over a lace tablecloth
all them kids hollering and bellering

this one boy not theirs
was being a Indin with a bow and arrow
nine years old name Jimmy Paul James
took and licked the stopper and shot
hit Mizrez Bullard
stuckt on the bottom of her arm
where it was hanging down
she was a fleshy worman
ever time she'd give that hair a pull
arrow'd jump up and down
kids commenced to yelling like sheetiron
        Shoot her again
        Don't shoot my mama
        Let me shoot it
        Shoot her on the floppers
her shirt was tore open in the front
until this one little girl
3 years old name Wanda Ann Bullard
got right in between them
looked straight up
sez mama Jimmy Paul James
done shot you with a error

them wormen let go of each other
stood right up
Lucille Bloodworth reached out

grapt that arrow and jerked it off
you could hear that rubberstopper pop
all the way down to my house
taken and broken it in half
Mizrez Bullard hollered oh my lard
I'm gone have a bruice big as a piepan
othern sez goddam ever ONE of you, who done that!
all them kids quit yelling right then
with their mouths hanging open

if he'd of just stood there
nobody would of ever known
neither one of them wormen could of told
which kids was theirs or the othern's
but Jimmy Paul James got coweyed
thrown them arrows straight up in the air
he would of strangled that bow to death
and it would of been deaf for life from the scream
if it had of been alive when he took off
for about 9 steps
broke the string when he thrown
it down so hard on the road
it sounded like the whole calvary
chasing one Indin after Custard
the way they took after him
down the blocks to his house
he ran in and locked the screendoor
shut the woodendoor
went round and pulled all the windershades down
got in his bed with a pillow over his head
they banged on the door and hollered
kids chucked clods at the house for a hour
only broke one window
but it wasn't nobody home
his mama and daddy worked for a living

sed they'd call Sheriff Red Floyd by god
they'd have him arrested and thrown in jail
with the murderers and the bootleggers
they'd put one of Charley Baker's idiots
in there with him and tell it
he had candy in his pockets
none of it done any good

they waited in the sun for him to come out
and finally when he didn't
they all went home
Lucille Bloodworth sez
you keep your kids away from my chirren
Mizrez Bullard sed
I don't care if I don't never see you again
she sez that's 2 days before
I'll lain eyes on you
sed you go to hell you whitetrash
sez so I can hear you hollering for icewater
all the way down the street
all them kids went in the house
and it was quiet that night
for oncet

3 days later
there's all them Bloodworth kids
lined up by the Bullard's car
their faces warshed and a clean shirt
Jimmy Paul James shoved in between them
to go to vacation Bible school
when Mizrez Bullard was cramming them in
one sed my mama told us
we didn't have to come back
till we had all the sandwich
and soda pop we wanted for dinner

so don't let you be in a hurry
Moses couldn't of made a dent
in them kids to see out the back winder
through the carmirror
looked like the Omaha hogtrain to Los Angeles
arms and legs hanging out the windows
wallering each other like a can of nightcrawlers
you could hear them half a mile off
singing
    Red and yellar black and white
    We love Jesust just for spite
    All the little chirren of the world

CLASSIFIED

I do professional quality FLORAL DESIGN if you will provide the materials and flowers. $6.00 to $12.00 per arrangement depending upon size. I am also selling some ORIGINAL POETRY which I wrote. Rights included. And; I do professional quality and HONEST HOUSE-CLEANING. $7.00 per hour. No more than four to six hours per day at this time. No windows. I also do fine detail NEEDLEWORK pieces. No silk. Finished. In layed. or unfinished. Can be used in a variety of lovely ways. Prices vary according to size and detail. You provide fabric or buy my samples when available. You can contact me reguarding any of the above between 9:30 A. M. and NOON: WEDNESDAY THROUGH SATURDAY at 68 NORTH 800th WEST STREET (the same street as North 8th West) REAR SINGLE SOUTHWEST APT. #S.E. (second of two doors. First is #A. Second and last is mine - #S. E.) Paragonah 84740. I have no go-betweens and no phone or message phone. ALSO. KITTENS (not for fund raising, experiments or bait) need homes. HUMANE TREAT-MENT a must. See only myself, MAVIS TITTLE, about all these matters.

WHAT HAPPENED WHEN BOBBY JACK COCKRUM TRIED TO BRING HOME A PIT BULLDOG
or
WHAT HIS DADDY SAID TO HIM THAT DAY

Son
let me tell you the story
of the man who saved
a baby grizzly bear
from a forest fire
and brought it home
nursed it
fed it
kept it like his own

And how the last thing
that man ever learned on earth
when it grown up
and he tried to keep it
out of the hog pen one morning
was the lesson
of what a grizzly bear
is at last

And it had
a final exam
he couldn't help
but pass

FAST

Janie Grace Gossett could outrun anybody
in the high school back then
before she had that car wreck
if she'd of been borned a boy
she could of been on the football team
except she's probley too little
her whole body was one piece of muscle
like a carpenter's crowbar
welded together without even a joint
you could of struct a match on her
you don't believe me?
a gopher match, anywhere

she'd wear bluejeans to the school on Fridays
like all the girls did oncet
it looked like two boar hogs in there
fighting it out in a chicken coop
when she walked past you with them britches on
Edgar McMahon down to the gin
sed if he could get cotton that tight
he'd put a 800 pound bale in a tow sack

then she took up with that sorry Harold Wayne Johnston
before he went blind and started being a gospelpreacher
he slobbered all over her
for about a half a year
until he ruint her reputation so he'd have a excuse
to move on to anothern
they sed she's going 80 miles a hour at least
when she went off the caprock
after he done it all and told

it was this one springtime
they's having the highschool track meet
whole town come out to see

if she could outrun Jimmy Ray Gary
who was gone graduate and go to the college
be on the team there
they had all the other races first
so we'd have to wait and see
finally it come to the last one
there she was in it
wearing this tight pink running outfit

that gun went off
first half she was out in front good
then he pulled up, all the otherns
was done behind by then
them two right beside each other the last part
everbody there was struck deaf and dumb
like they's on the road to Damascus
their mouths hanging open like it was a vision
for just a second or 2 that day turned into pear jelly
her body melted into that running suit
looked like she was bald naked running wide open
only one othern seemed to be moving
besides them 2 was Harold Wayne Johnston
running down to the finish line to grab her
like she's a holstein cow right in front of everbody
probley thought she done all that just for him

I don't think anybody could tell you
who won that footrace
we lost that in the watching
but we all had words for it
that we known by heart
I heard my mouth say Amazing Grace
we all remember R. B. McCravey hollering
that there's poetry in motion
Ollie McDougald sed it was a religious experience

but Leonard Tittle who was already preaching on weekends
and had both of them in his class of algebrar
sez right out loud
nosir gentlemen you are all wrong
that was Grace abounding to the chief of sinners

THE LEGEND OF THE MONSTER IN TWO DRAW

Place where we'd swim on posted land
we had to cross the Bird Ranch to get to
was called 2 Draw back then
before them 3 boys seen that creature in the water
and the town had to build a swimming pool
for it finally to stop the 2nd Coming
and keep Kay Stokes from bankrupting the county
then they name it Stokes Monster Lagoon

them boys was fishing without permission
when it got hot on a day
so they could put their fishing poles
with a rock on them
went down to the other side by the deep end
where the tree limb hung over with the rope
like all the other towns have there
so they could go swimming
and practice hanging theirselves
had all the clothes off ready to jump in
when it was a miracle
that tank water commenced to churning up
like spoilt beer foaming out the still boiler
all this moss come off the bottom 15 foot
you could see crappie fishes running down
to the other end and they sed
they never knew it was so many
turtles in there everwhere getting out
these two black humps come up in the water
on top banging and sloshing but no yelling
at first they was about 3 foot across
after a week it was up to 4 or 5 with eyeballs
and arms down under the water they couldn't see
then just sunk back down
it might of got real quiet after that
nobody knows because them boys

didn't wait to find out
Billy Ray Bilberry got almost 2 miles
down the road before he remembered
his clothes hiding under a rock by the tree
he squatted in some bushes that didn't cover him up
while them other 2 run on in to town
till he got so sunburnt because he was redheaded
he looked like a duroc hog with water blisters
on its ast and freckles that went all the way down
years later when he's grown up
his wife sed they's all over him and stayed for good
because of what he seen in that tank

one of the otherns Bubba Bowen I think
had on only drawers and a tee shirt running
but called Billy Ray's house anyway
his daddy had to come get him with the car
he wouldn't go back he's so ascairt
none of them boys would for a week
somebody else stoled the clothes
and all the fishing poles they sed
one even had a catfish on
them boys didn't even care about no more
they couldn't of been more famous
if they'd of been killed or went blind on bad whiskey
they broke in and stoled from a shiner
in one day everbody around known
by a week it got so bad they had to
call a town meeting so they could
keep all the people scared to death about it
for something to worry and call each other liars over
besides the churchhouse and town council
A. N. Lucas was mayor back then
but he couldn't even get them to shut up
so he could call it to order

106

Mizrez Fortune who was arredy 80 by then
sed it was dark shadows
crawling in the alleys she'd seen at night
probley out there to rape her in the dark
while she's looking at the neighbor's windows
with her binoculars all alone
without a husband she could really use now
2 of them hired hands over to the No Lazy S
sed they'd swear to a oath
it was flying saucers mutilated
42 head of cattle across the nation
that the insurance had the responsibility to pay for
and cut all their privates off
Kay Stokes had wrote their testimony out
on a piece of paper for them to read
then Coy Stribling stood on a chair
with his blue Newtestament they give his kids
up to the junior high school before they quit
and run off in his hand reading out loud
about the Nicolaitanes which he hated
but we hadn't met yet so we had to wait awhile
he read how it was a bottomless pit with smoke
of the furnace by reason of the dark air
and scorpions having hair as the hair of wormen
and then a dragon casting out a flood from his mouth
with the arms of Gideon
which was a prophesy of the Lord which sez
he's gonna show unto us Jeremiah's whore
coming up out of the water
with one hand full of abomination
and the filthiness of her fornication
in the othern

well that got even the Baptists
cause we known that's what them boys

been talking about
they couldn't deny it
it was a sign from God Coy sed and read
the 2nd Coming was at hand
to wipe out all the dogs and whoremongers
and murderers and idolaters
and whosoever loveth and maketh a lie
right there in the book word for word
spewing hot and cold out the mouth of Jesust
he had us all going straight to hell
if we didn't get right to the churchhouse
with money for the collection plate
it was wormen bawling and men
promising to pay up debts
and stay out of the beer joints in the flats
all over in there
one of them 3 boys was about to have
a espiscoleptic fit he was so ascairt
from what he'd done that very day
he sworn out loud he'd cut the palm of his hand out
with a butcher knife or a meat axe
before he'd ever touch hisself with it again
he was sure he was the reason it happened
cause the Lord had been watching
him do it in the garden
he known it'd be white hairs of the heathen
growing all over and out it by judgement day
he could feel hisself going blind

some of them Pennycostals was ready
to go to their churchhouse and get snakes
and jars of poison for testimony
sed all them people was so worked up
they's ready for it by then
and the fat womern could jump the benches

108

started clapping singing Jesust saves
until A. N. Lucas finally got Sheriff Floyd
to get Coy Stribling down off that chair
and that Newtestament in a drawer
so he'd shut up and they could have a meeting
and whoever else wouldn't close his mouth
would have to leave until he was calt on
then sed what do we do?
Coy Stribling hollers Acts 2:38
R. B. McCravey sez that's it
I'm gone kill that sonofabitch
but Sheriff Floyd wouldn't let him
it was too many witnesses
they sed Coy could either leave right now
or not say another word until he had permission
R. B. moved over behind him
taken out his pocketknife and started
cutting on his warts and fingernails
shaving the hair on his wrists and arms
Coy didn't say no more

Mayor sez we got the problem of a hysterical community
over a unexplained happening
we have to get to the bottom of
by using our common sense
so what DO we do now?
everbody in there had a rumor and a idea
some sed build a fence with barbwore
and electricity around that tank
Eugene Cummings sed a fence like that
never held hogs in even
if they'd get out whatall's in that water'd find a way too
come find us in the night
Mattie Lou Collier sed she was gone buy her
a shotgun and keep it in her closet

Mizrez Fortune sed oh no
you got it all too crowded in there
it'd be better under the bed
where she could get to it
on the lefthand side by her blue houseshoes
Ellis Britton sed throw dynamites in the tank
see if it'd come up and we'd line the banks
on both sides with rifles from the 1st amendment
shoot acrost the water
at each other to kill it
then it was a motion from Beulah K. Bird
who was proud it happened on No Lazy S ground
to tear out the dam and drain the tank
so it wouldn't have no place to be
that we thought was a pretty good idea
until Kay Stokes stood up and sed
nosir gentlemen you are NOT
gone tear out no goddam dam on my property
while I'm alive I guarantee it for a fact
when the District Attorney Waymon Gamblin sez
it was in the interest and benefit
of the community Kay Stokes sed
any one of you sets 1 foot on my ranch
by that tank I'll personally
have my Mexican hired hand shoot you
in the inarrest and benefit of the community
in the head or worst for trespassing
I'll take ever penny I own
out of the bank right on that day
this whole county will go under on the spot
because I own that bank
I'll buy a bankrupt sale
and bid on ever bit of it you think's yours
won't none of you ever get
one thing of it back so help me Joshera

Beulah K. Bird can go straight to hell
if she thinks she's getting one drop of my water
you can write that down in the book
for judgement day

wasn't nobody sed nothing after that
Kay Stokes had that whole town by the short hairs
we known he'd do it like he sed
wasn't nothing else to add up
then he sed if it's the Lard pissed off
like your Reverent Coy sez
well I don't blame him
it's time you stopped electing republicans
and trespassing on private property
you keep your ast and your kids where it's posta be
none of this wouldn't happen
so if the Lard's got a problem
he can take it up with me
I done built a fence around that tank
now you quit crawling through it
stirring up things isn't none of your business
and none of this won't ever happen again
whatall's in that tank is on my land
if it aint human it belongs to me
if it is it probley does anyway
I don't want to hear nobody in here
even think about it again it's mine
so you get on home and watch television
that's all you dismissed
he set down and stared at us
until we figured out he was through talking
that was permission for us to leave
his courthouse so we did

111

it must of worked
nothing else happened
somebody put up a sign sed Monster Lagoon
by the fence that he kept
after he put Stokes on top
so they'd remember it was his
and spoilt the joke they'd made
a year later we didn't even think about it
that much any more except for kids
town finally passed a bond
to build a swimming pool
for something to do
of a summer when it was too hot
wouldn't nobody go out to 2 Draw no more on a bet

it was 4 years later
my cousin by marriage to Tilda Sims
was working for No Lazy S Ranch
had to go down there to pull a cow
stuck in mud with a pickup out
worked 1/2 a day getting her loose
another 2 hours
keeping her from going right back in
had to herd her down to the one by the blue gate
on hardscrabble where she couldn't
find her a place to sink in to her armpits
getting a drink of water
sed while he's out there in that shinery
chasing that cow he about had a heart attack
run right up on this snapping turtle
looking like the biggest bloated baby elephant
he'd ever saw in his life
sed you couldn't of covered it up
with a number 12 warshtub
if it would of bit him

it'd take his whole leg off
just setting there by the tank
staring at him in the sunshine

Kay Stokes when he heard
calt him in sed
son I'm gone give you fifteen dollars
to never tell nobody what you seen out there
that turtle is my property
and I'm buying the memory of it
right out of your mind
I own that too
I hear you ever told 1 person what you seen
you won't never work in this state again
even for Bryant Williamson
you better believe me good
you go buy your wife supper
at Lela's Cafe on me tonight
and don't never remember nothing
about this ever again
so that's what he did
for over a year
until him and my brother got personally drunk
one night and he told him in confidence
by swearing him to god he wouldn't never tell nobody else
but he told me the next day
pretty soon we all knew
but we also knew we couldn't tell
it was the official town secret
known only to Kay Stokes and by us

it didn't matter
we arredy had what we were gone believe
learned by heart
we had the swimming pool by then

them boys was famous
Coy Stribling took credit for stopping the 2nd Coming
with his testimony before the Lord
that doubled the collection plate at his churchhouse
for almost a month so he could trade his car in on a new used or
and we had a place to take the girlfriends
on a Friday night for wallering
where they'd have a excuse to be too ascairt
to get out and walk back to town in the dark
even at that age
just like religion and town council
that's there to hold the multitudes together
we known it's some legends and opinions
you can't let facts get in the way of

RIGHTEOUS

TOM CHRISTENSON

PARAGONAH — Tom Wayne Christenson, age 82, passed away on Nov 28, 1994, at his home in Paragonah. He was born Nov 26, 1912, in Hickory Flat, Miss., to A. Johnston and Marjorie Mael Christensen. He graduated from Searcy Jr High School Ark, then moved near Paragonah where he farmed and lived alone. Reverend Boyde M. Chilingham stated that he was a very kind person and was so loved by all who knew him. He placed his faith in church and the Lord.

Funeral services are Tuesday, Dec. 1 at the Paragonah Assembly for God at 2. Burial will be at Terace Mound Cemetery under the direction of Huffman Mortuary Rufus Garner officiating.

He sed the world
it wasn't no fit place
to live in for decent people
spent his life watching
it get worst and worst

ever year the Lard waited
to make itself known
and burn it all up with hellfore
till he got so old
he couldn't wait no more
so he died in bed alone

115

EULOGY AFTER THE FACT
or
REFLECTIONS ON A GIFT FROM A MAGI

Matthew 25:40

it was a day in August
after the County Fair
this boy was walking a 40 pound shoat backwards
he won in a greasepig chase
up a gravel road
with a bucket over its head
9 years old when Bryant Williamson
drove his pickup right there
rolt down the window
spit Brown Garrett snuf on the ground
sed what's that hog?
boy sez it's mine
he sed I can see that
it's the one with the bucket on its head
where you going to with it?
boy sed from that cedarpost yonder
by the powerpole 4 more miles

Bryant Williamson asked him
hasn't nobody come along this way?
boy sed just one truck
from No Lazy S
it never stopped just honk to get by
Bryant Williamson sed I don't mean to be polite
and speak ill of them I wish was dead
but them's Kay Stokes hired hands
and he is one sorry sonofabitch
I'll testify that to a oath
boy sed I know it

Bryant Williamson sed hogs are like Democrats
they won't lead and they won't foller

unless they real hungry
and you got a full bucket in your hand
you might as well put it
on their head and go backwards
boy sed I know it
Bryant Williamson sed you want a ride?
boy sed if you aint got no wheelbarrer
that sounds fine

him and that old man
wallered that hog by its tail and ears squalling
to be heard 12 miles like a insane man
whose wife lost his mama's handkerchief
into the back of his truck
tied its feet up with baliwore
so he could set up front
and look out the window driving
4 miles home

Bryant Williamson sed that's a fine Christmas pig
boy sed nosir it aint
I'm having babies with it
he look back at that barrow
say I believe we may have another star
rising in the east by then
boy sez I know it
never sed no more
drove him and his pig home
unloaded them and got it in the pen
fixed a gate to hold it in

next part I have to make a guess at
but he must of drove
a hundred miles that night
to find a black listed 40 pound gilt pig
twin of that greased barrow

how he got her swapped in that pen
without waking up that boy
I didn't find out for 10 years
until the day they had his funeral
R. B. McCravey told me
he bought a 5 gallon bucket
of sour mash right out of his still
so he could get 2 pigs drunk enough
to load them without a squolt
sed if anybody ever ast one word about it
he'd see they got sued from both sides
and died with unpaid insurance
that was a fact

that boy had his pig moren 9 years
she farreled almost 200 head of babies
got him raised and through the FFA
eat up ever beet in the garden 4 times
and I believe that bucket's still around
hanging on a nail in the barnloft
if it's a need for it

they say it takes 3 turns
done for the doing and kept a secret
to get to heaven
Bryant Williamson was crooked and rotten
as a doughty aspen
Kay Stokes told that to everybody
who would listen to hear it
and he was too rich to argue about it with
but I know personal of 2 he had on account
as long as Kay Stokes aint the goodlord yet
it's at least a small chance
he might of made it

RHAPSODY FOR THE GOOD NIGHT
CHRISTMAS EVE '94

Matthew 8:22

1

> *Libations*
> *liquid and flowing*
> *beneath the knees of the gods*

Strangest man ever was E. U. Washburn
his bible name was Ethopian Eunuch
come from that family opened the book
whatall was there got named
had Cephas Peter that we called C. P. or Junior
and hated because he went to school studying typewriter
come back educated where he known
the meaning of life and wrote it in a 4 page paper
for the college
loved to tell about it but never got the idea
wasn't nobody listening
the other brother Phillip Chariot
we called Bubber because he had his harelip
so he watched television until Floyd Scott
got fired at Christenson's Brothers
they hired Bubber to make coffee and clean office
nurse tried to not let them name him that
but Dr. Tubbs sed go ahead
they'll call him by the letters anyway
they did so E. U. worked at the graveyard
digging and tending with Jesus Salinas

he's the baby so they raised him with Bubber
probley not talking a whole lot
when he's grown up most people or some
never known he could say nothing at all

some sed he was deaf and dumb
addled but they's wrong all 3 ways
he mostly didn't like to talk
he'd come to the cafe by hisself
set and listen and nod

oncet it wasn't no place open to be with people
I went back to where he was in the booth
sed E. U. can I set here with you drinking coffee?
looked at me but I never set down till he nod
sed how ya'll anyway? he lipped justfine
1st time I heard him say anything
when we through not saying nothing
for a 1/2 hour listening to the otherns
I sed I gotta go you need a ride?
I had to drive past the graveyard to the farm
he never sed nothing then either
got up paid his bill
went out got in my truck
both of us drove to work that way
for moren a year till I got a job
at the sawmill and had to leave early

he talk soft
couldn't play no radio to hear him
when he sed something at all

sed them's the hardest that day when I sez
it's bad about that Reuben Jimenez boy
who was in the Boy Scouts until he
died of the appendicitis when he's 14 in high school
on the operating table without waking up
it was a month later before he sed more
that was what opened the gate

sed that boy isn't figured out he's gone yet
I dunno what to do about it
they buriet him in the wrong place
isn't nobody there to help him or tell him what to do
I sez whar?
didn't have no idea what he's talking about
he sed that Jimenez boy
longest speech he'd sed up to then
I had to think for almost a week
couldn't make it add I sez how do you know? then
without asting what? he sed
I can tell

2
nightbird
and the hum of pickup tires
on hardscrabble

I listen
behind the mockingbird behind the wind
behind the sound a taproot makes
working its way down to water
past that I can hear them
theygn hear me too
if they want to
but they mostly don't
sometimes I talk
not to them mostly
to myself to the wind
to the field mouse under the plastic grass
in the shed by the mesquite tree
sometimes they pay attention
it's other ways too
like how they settle in to stay
or don't

Leona Huffington there
has her back to her husband
won't talk to him
but doesn't even know
he don't care

Baucis and Philemon Rojas had both
sed look for a bright spring sunrise they'd be
in bed sleeping in their morning garden
next to each other past tomorrow's dawn
Jesus thought the one plot was fine with the
headstone with one name but both in the one
red box under a blanket dressed that way
he wasn't sure of but they'd planned it through
it was what they wore their first night they wrote
so Rufus did just like they said then we
planted on both sides of their place the two
rose stalks they'd raised by their garden window
roses bloom now over the stone in a
bow bright red as Easter morning sunshine

that other rosebush over there by Tommy Malouf
it's growing right out the palm of his hand
and in that flowerplant it's a mockingbird every day
pointing itself right at
Janie Grace Gossett who got killed
in the car wreck in high school singing
aint never a weed grown at her place
that Malouf boy give her flowers and the song
she settled right in knowing she belonged

some out there's helpless
like that Reverent Brother Strayhan
found out it aint at all
like what he been told to think
now it's too late

biggest surprises
was Ellis Britton and Kay Stokes
everbody thought Ellis he wouldn't never
fit in cause he's so mean
he was the happiest I ever seen
found out we's all wrong
he never hated the people
he hated the living
Mistah Stokes now on the other hand
he hated us all
so he aint never settled in
probley won't
at least as long as Jesus is watching
can't get used to not being in charge

on a night of a full moon that comes on a payday
I seen Jesus out there with him getting drunk
telling him about all the times he come
thrown him and his family off the No Lazy S
sworn at him in front of his chirren and dog
now he sez well now Mr. Kay Stokes I believe
I'll go fishing down to the tank by the blue gate
catch me that big catfish they say down there
so what you think about that Mr. Kay Stokes dead man?

I'll swear I seen
one thousand dandelion weeds pop up
all over that grave in a night
when he's been listening to Jesus
whole grave come up 3 inches
he's trying so hard to get out
I rakes him back down in the morning sunshine

Ellis Britton settled
in 2 weeks or a month
so fast we never paid it mind

when the otherns out there saw he's ready
they started the rumor
we all have to come back do it again
he slunk down deep and low as he could
holding on tight
took 2 wheelbarrows to level him up
he just fine
a satisfied mind

3

Music is silence.
The reason we have the notes
is to emphasize the silence.
          Dizzy Gillespie

owl say who
preacher say whar
Rufus say here
me and Jesus
we start building
a hole in the ground
he sing
Lead me gently home father

dying
crying
singing
preaching
praying
bringing
burying

then we all begin
the next beginning
covering
forgetting
remembering
calling
neglecting
loving
hating
moving on along

out here
back there
all the same:
wind blow
bird sing
grass grow
churchbell ring

nightime quiet
it all sink in

4

romantic interlude
of a windy afternoon:
sunlight and elmshadow on stone

year later Christmastime
I seen E. U. of a morning sed set down
we drank coffee till the otherns left
he sed I got that Jimenez boy settled
I sez you did? he sed yas
but it almost costed me the farm

wasn't nobody heping
they done forgot about him
all alone and scairt
down there whar it aint no time
I had to extablish a reason
they had to hep him in

I known if I could get Mistah Kay Stokes
working against my case
they'd all the rest hep that boy
I sed aint we all from the same clay?
he sed mebbe that's so boy
but it aint no jug is a vase

I sed does a man
have to come down there early
to set that boy to rest at home
cause if you aint gone do it
then I'll have to
Jesus'll clean your yard alone

that's whatall it took
Ruby Patrick sed to her own daddy
neither one's porcelain so there you go
Janie Grace Gossett sed whar's that boy?
Tommy Malouf sed I'll find him
mockingbird flown to the Rojas rose

it was a whispering in the grass
in the trees in the wind whar? sed Ellis
whar's he at whar's he at they sed donde donde
mockingbird took him the song
in words he could understand
in a day the prodigal son he come home

5

in his hand a glass
filled with the moon
        drowned in branchwater
or
what E. U. said
    on Christmas day

here's to the newyear
and here's to the old one
and here's to the place in between
the sunrise and the morning
between the midnight and the fullmoon
that place
between the owlcall and the mockingbird
between the roostercrow and the last henlight
under the trees under the rose
under the grass under the shadow of a footprint
that place
where all the naming and the doing
where all the listening and talking
where all the lying and the truesaying
where all the storying and the singing
where all the words theyselves
which is the first and last thing of all
slide into quiet
that dark sleeping place they can call home
just between the dreamsay
and the realsay of it all
that place
where those who know
who live there
know that without the making and remembering and telling
to help us all get on along
it aint no difference or worth finally
in none of it at all

127

E. U. WASHBURN'S STORY:
UNCLE ABE

I have not wasted my life
   –Richard Shelton, "Desert Water"

Genesis 17:7

1

Oncet when I was a boy
a walking man come
to town twicet every year
folks didn't know who he was
name him Uncle Abe
sed he was lost and wandering
in his own mind
a harmless old thing just passing by

carried this paper bag in his hand
no child or cat can not find out what's in
I sidled him in the gravel road sez
Mister Man, what you got in that paper sack?

he turnt round looked me up and down
like a rooster hypnotized
by a line in the sand
sed Master Boy, I'll tell you what I brought
but you answer me first one thing
you say how many years your mama's got
I told and he sed not enuf
tell me your grandmama's home
I sed she aint she's dead and gone

2

he say
    I was a almost whole live grown up boy oncet
    like you walking along soon
    had me a paper sack of store bought candy
    going down the road
    after work at the cotton gin
    girlchild womern on her poach call me say
    Mister Man, what you got in that possible sack?
    come here show me right now
    patted beside her where for me to set
    I come to her she say what you bring?
    I shook all over
    she was beautiful as churchhouse sin
    I felt as ugly as the real thing

    she eat a piece without asking
    I known deep in my paper sack it was
    one chocolate covenant hiding to be last
    pretty soon we almost racing
    eating that candy so fast
    she lay one smiling piece on her tongue
    with her finger say come here
    put her mouth on mine
    she pass me that seed
    take it back and again
    till the covenant was gone
    then so was she
    all but the memory

    I had me one wife, son,
    four good chirren grown up
    left and gone
    but never nothing

like that day since come along
now I got *hope* and *mebbe*
and then whatall time's left
this paperbag of sweet candy with one covenant
for her somewhere waiting
if I'm so blessed

3

he told me his story that day
again every time since twice a year
till the day he didn't come here
I never stopped remembering
the promise I made
to never have to say
I got no more of my life to waste
I still try to look
down every street
at every porch
every old walking man's face
every shadowed place

4

oncet mama say
you don't be shiftless boy
don't you daydream your life away
pretty soon you be walking lonesome
empty head and pocket
like that crazy Uncle Aberham
kicking rocks down the gravel road

I sed oh Mama Mama
don't even promise that might be so
it's a whole live world
inside that lucky man
you and all the rest of this town
don't even know
one sweet covenant
you can't never understand

ACKNOWLEDGMENTS

Some of William Kloefkorn's poems have appeared in the following publications: *North Dakota Quarterly*, *Georgia Review*, *Witness*, *Tar River Poetry*, *Nebraska Poets Calendar*, *Harper's*, *New Orleans Review*, *South Dakota Review*, *Zone 3*, *Ellipsis*, *Midwest Quarterly*, *Laurel Review*, and *Hurakan*. Some of them were also reprinted in an anthology of Nebraska Poets, *Wellsprings*, edited by Susanne George.

Some of David Lee's poems have appeared in the following publications: *Weber Studies*, *Story*, *Puerto del Sol*, *Poetry East*, *Ellipsis*, *Witness*, *Tailwind*, *Etudes*, *Mummy Mountain Press*, and *Quarterly West*.

ABOUT THE AUTHORS

William Kloefkorn, Professor of English at Nebraska Wesleyan in Lincoln, is the author of several collections of poetry, among them *Alvin Turner As Farmer*, *Houses and Beyond*, *Drinking the Tin Cup Dry*, *Platte Valley Homestead*, *Dragging Sand Creek for Minnows*, and *Going Out, Coming Back*. In 1982 the Nebraska Unicameral by proclamation named him State Poet. He and his wife Eloise have four children and nine grandchildren.

David Lee lives quietly in St. George and/or Pine Valley, Utah, with Jan, Jon, and Jodee, where he scribbles and wanders the country roads and trails, all at about the same rate and pace. His collection of poems, *My Town*, won the 1995 Western States Book Award.